Workbook

BACKPACK 3

Second Edition

Mario Herrera · Diane Pinkley

Contributing Writer
Donna Schaffer

PEARSON
Longman

Backpack 3, Second Edition
Workbook

Pearson Education, 10 Bank Street, White Plains, NY 10606, USA

Staff credits: The people who made up the *Backpack 3* Workbook team, representing editorial, production, design, and manufacturing, are Rhea Banker, Carol Brown, Sarah Bupp, Tracey Cataldo, Gina DiLillo, Christine Edmonds, Maria Pia Marrella, Linda Moser, Diane Pinkley, Edie Pullman, Nicole Santos, Susan Saslow, and Andrew Vaccaro.

Text composition: TSI Graphics
Text font: 14 pt HSP Helvetica Text
Illustration credits: Aubrey, Meg, 2, 33; Berlin, Rose Mary, 3, 6, 44; Bridy, Dan, 2, 3, 5, 33, 37, 48, 56, 62, 74, 85; Catanese, Donna, 4, 43; Dammer, Mike, 12, 22, 32, 88; Flanagan, Kate, 15, 24, 26, 38, 48, 78, 86; Gott, Barry, 1, 71; Harris, Marty, 8, 10, 23, 28, 37, 53, 64, 65; Kizlauskas, Diana, 31, 63; McClurkan, Rob, 36; Mendenhall, Cheryl, 21; Miranda, Hugo, 91, 92, 94, 95, 97, 99; Montiel, Javier, 8, 13, 14, 18, 25, 33, 35, 48, 51, 52, 54, 56, 61, 68, 84, 85; O'Neill, Sean, 5, 28, 45, 54, 73, 75; Pye, Trevor, 66, 68; Roca, Paul Eric, 41, 81; Tejido, Jomike, 11

Photo credits: l = left, c = center, r = right, t = top, b = bottom
Page 27 ©AFP/Corbis; 34 ©Nicole Duplaix/National Geographic Image Collection; 52 ©Superstock, Inc.; 58 (paint, medicine, pins, soap, chips, perfume, sandpaper) ©The Image Works, (kitten) ©PhotoDisc, Inc., (truck) ©Lynton Gardiner/Dorling Kindersley Picture Library; 77 (br) ©Kit Houghton/Bettman/Corbis, (tl) ©George Shelley/Corbis, (tc) Jeff Greenberg/PhotoEdit, Inc., (tr) ©Chris Carroll/Corbis, (bl) ©Jose Luis Pelaez, Inc./Corbis, (bc) ©Lawrence Migdale; 83 ©Chris North; Cordaiy Photo Library/Corbis; 84 ©Digital Vision/Getty Images, (tr) ©Michael Newman/PhotoEdit, Inc., (bl) ©Eric O'Connell/Taxi/Getty Images, (br) ©Comstock; 87 (tl) ©Dave King/Dorling Kindersley Picture Library, (tr) ©Marianne Henderson, (bl) ©Dallas and John Heaton/Corbis, (br) ©Webistan/Corbis.

ISBN-13: 978-0-13-245104-8
ISBN-10: 0-13-245104-2

...ted in the United States of America
...–V011—13 12 11

Contents

1 From Morning to Night 1

2 Helping Hands 11

3 Pen Pals 21

4 Amazing Animals 31

5 Rain or Shine 41

6 Our Five Senses 51

7 A World of Food 61

8 In Shape! 71

9 Puppets 81

Sound and Spelling Handbook . . . 91

Review 100

Grammar and Writing 106

TRACK 03

1 **Listen and write. Draw lines to match.**

Exactly Ed

> Every day at exactly ___6:45___,
>   Ed gets out of bed.

Not _____, or 6:46,
    because he's Exactly Ed.

Every day at exactly _____,
    Ed gets ready to go.

> He washes his face, combs his hair,
>   and gets dressed—
> never fast and never slow.

He does the same things
    at the same time every day.
Because he's Exactly Ed,
    it just has to be that way.

> Every day at exactly _____,
>   Ed eats his breakfast.

> Then he brushes his teeth,
>   and he walks to school.
> So at _____ he sits at his desk.

(Chorus)

2 Match the times.

1. eleven forty-five
2. one thirty-five
3. eight ten
4. seven twenty
5. five fifty
6. three thirty

3 What time is it now? Write and draw.

_____

4 Point to the clocks on this page. Ask and say the time.

Excuse me. What time is it, please?

It's 11:45.

| before | I take a shower **before** school. | shower—7:30 | school—8:00 |
| after | I play soccer **after** school. | soccer—5:00 | dinner—6:00 |

5 Write *before* or *after*.

1. I brush my teeth ___before___ school.

2. I play video games _____ school.

3. I get dressed _____ school.

4. I eat dinner _____ school.

5. I do my homework _____ school.

6 Write about you.

1. What do you do before you eat breakfast?

   _____

2. What do you do after you eat breakfast?

   _____

3. What do you do after you get home from school?

   _____

4. What do you do before you eat dinner?

   _____

5. What do you do after you watch TV?

   _____

I	I **wash** my face before I **brush** my teeth.
He	My brother **brushes** his teeth before he **washes** his face.
She	My sister **brushes** her teeth before she **washes** her face.

7 **Look. Complete the sentences.**

| 7:15 | 7:30 | 7:40 | 7:45 | 8:10 |

1. Jesse gets dressed after he ___gets up___.

2. Jesse gets dressed before he _____.

3. Jesse combs his hair after he _____.

4. Jesse combs his hair before he _____.

5. Jesse eats breakfast after he _____.

6. Jesse eats breakfast before he _____.

8 **Answer the questions about Jesse.**

1. What time does Jesse get dressed?

   Jesse gets dressed at 7:30.

2. What time does he comb his hair?

   _____

3. What time does he eat breakfast?

   _____

4. What time does he brush his teeth?

   _____

9 **Look. Write.**

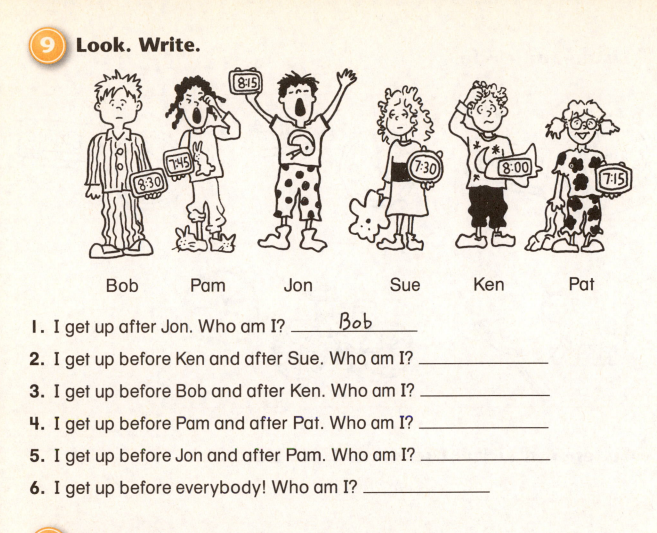

| Bob | Pam | Jon | Sue | Ken | Pat |

1. I get up after Jon. Who am I? _____Bob_____

2. I get up before Ken and after Sue. Who am I? _____

3. I get up before Bob and after Ken. Who am I? _____

4. I get up before Pam and after Pat. Who am I? _____

5. I get up before Jon and after Pam. Who am I? _____

6. I get up before everybody! Who am I? _____

10 **What time does Lazy Susan get up?**
Find and circle the time. Color.

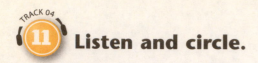

Listen and circle.

TRACK 05

12 Listen and write. Use words from the box.

After School

I work hard in school all day,

so after school it's time to _____play_____.

I go and get my ball and _____,

and my favorite baseball hat.

I meet my friends at five o'clock sharp,

and then play baseball 'til it's _____.

I go back home to watch _____,

and then eat dinner with my family.

I do my _____ and help my mom,

and then it's nine—the day is gone.

So as I go to bed I say,

tomorrow is another _____!

bat
dark
day
homework
play
TV

6

Betty Backwards

 13 **Read** *Betty Backwards.* **Find the answers in the story. Write.**

1. When does Betty get up?

   Betty gets up at ten o'clock at night.

2. What does Betty do after she brushes her teeth?

   _____

3. What does Betty do before school?

   _____

4. What does Betty do before she eats her vegetables?

   _____

5. How does Betty read a story?

   _____

14 **Check (✔) *yes* or *no*.**

	Yes	No
1. Does Betty wear pajamas out to play?	✔	☐
2. Do you wear pajamas out to play?	☐	☐
3. Does Betty go to school on weekends?	☐	☐
4. Do you go to school on weekends?	☐	☐
5. Does Betty walk her cat after school?	☐	☐
6. Do you walk your cat after school?	☐	☐
7. Does Betty have dinner before she goes to bed?	☐	☐
8. Do you have dinner before you go to bed?	☐	☐
9. Is Betty like you?	☐	☐

Review

15 **Match clocks and times. Draw lines.**

1. eleven twenty-five
2. six fifty-five
3. nine ten
4. two thirty

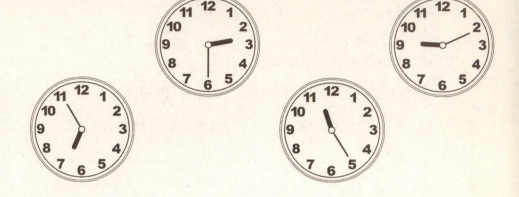

16 **Look. Answer the questions.**

Rolando's Saturday

9:00 in the morning   2:15 in the afternoon   6:30 in the evening

1. What time does Rolando walk his dog?

   _____

2. What does Rolando do in the afternoon?

   _____

3. What does Rolando do before he rides his bike?

   _____

4. What does Rolando do in the evening?

   _____

Cut-out Activity ✂- - - - - - - - - - - - - - - - -

A. **Look at the times.**
   Write other times.
B. **Cut out the cards and**
   glue them in the boxes.
C. **Find a partner.**
D. **Ask and answer questions**
   about what time you do things.

What time do
you get dressed?

I get dressed
at seven o'clock.

In the morning

	→ 7:30	→ 8:15	→
_____			_____

In the afternoon

	→ 3:00	→ 4:30	→
_____			_____

brush teeth and wash face	comb or brush hair	do homework	eat breakfast
eat lunch	feed a pet	get dressed	get up
go to school	play a (video) game	play baseball, soccer, or tennis	read a book
ride a bike	take a shower or a bath	use a computer	watch TV

Students create activity time lines for the activities on the strips. They
write other times they do things and cut and glue the activities in the
boxes. They ask and answer questions about each other's schedules.

TRACK 06

1 **Listen and write. Draw lines to match.**

Helpers

There are many helping hands
in my family.
We like to help each other out
in our community.

_____ keep us safe—
   police officers, too.
My uncle John's a firefighter.
What does your uncle do?

_____ help to keep us fed—
   chefs and waiters, too.
My father is a farmer.
What does your father do?

(Chorus)

_____ help us learn a lot—
   TV reporters, too.
My mother is a teacher.
What does your mother do?

(Chorus)

2 Write. Use words from the box.

barber   coach   mail carrier
salesperson   secretary   waiter

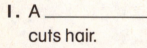

1. A _____
cuts hair.

2. A _____
serves food.

3. A _____
brings the mail.

4. A _____
sells clothes.

5. A _____
types letters.

6. A _____
teaches sports.

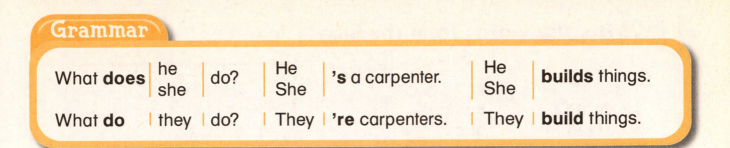

| What **does** | he
she | do? | He
She | **'s** a carpenter. | He
She | **builds** things. |
| What **do** | they | do? | They | **'re** carpenters. | They | **build** things. |

3 **Look and write.**

Taro and His Family

1. What does Taro's grandfather do? He's _a barber_____.
   He cuts hair.

2. What does Taro's mother do? She's _____.
   She designs buildings.

3. What does Taro's uncle do? He's _____.
   He helps sick people.

4. What do Taro's aunts do? They're _____.
   They help sick animals.

5. What does Taro do? He's _____.
   He goes to school.

4 Write. Use words from the box.

brings	designs
fixes	goes
helps	writes

This is Linda and her family. Her family likes to help the community. Her father is a vet. He (1) _____ sick animals. Her mother is a dentist. She (2) _____ teeth. Her aunt is a journalist. She (3) _____ stories for newspapers. Her uncle is an architect. He (4) _____ buildings. Her cousin is a mail carrier. He (5) _____ the mail. Linda is a student. She (6) _____ to school.

Grammar

Who helps us live in comfort?
Plumbers do, **because** they put running hot and cold water in our homes.

5 Write.

1. Who helps us get information?

_____

_____

2. Who helps us stay healthy?

_____

_____

6 **Look and write. Use words from the box.**

1.

2.

3.

4.

5.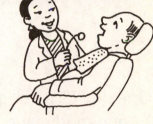

6.

| architect | dentist | firefighter |
| mail carrier | plumber | vet |

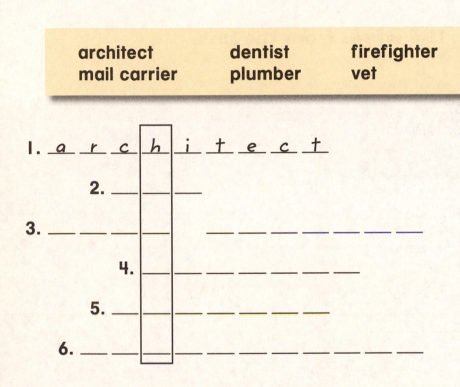

1. a r c h i t e c t
2. _ _ _ _ _
3. _ _ _ _ _ _ _ _ _ _ _
4. _ _ _ _ _ _
5. _ _ _ _ _ _ _
6. _ _ _ _ _ _ _ _ _

What's the secret word in the box?

_____

7 **Write about your family. Draw and color.**

This person is my _____

_____.

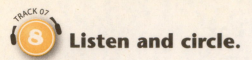

8 **Listen and circle.**

1. nurses   exercise instructors   carpenters

2. journalists   firefighters   barbers

3. farmers   dentists   mail carriers

4. secretaries   computer programmers   coaches

9 **Listen and write. Use words from the box.**

astronaut	doctor
singer	soccer star
TV reporter	

One Day

One day I'll be all grown up
and ready for a job.

Maybe I'll be a _____
like my uncle Bob.

Or maybe I'll be a _____
and sign my name for fans.

Or maybe I'll be a _____
in a famous band.

Or maybe I'll be an _____
and fly in outer space.

Or maybe I'll be a _____
like my cousin Grace.

What will you be? Draw.

A Circus Family

10 **Read *A Circus Family*. Check *yes* or *no*.**

	Yes	No
1. Natasha works with her family in the circus.	☐	☐
2. Her grandmother swings on a trapeze.	☐	☐
3. Her grandfather is an electrician.	☐	☐
4. Her mother can turn cartwheels and jump very high.	☐	☐
5. Her uncle is a clown. He makes people sad.	☐	☐
6. Her aunt is a juggler.	☐	☐

11 **Write numbers.**

What circus jobs do you like? (1 = the best job 6 = the worst job)

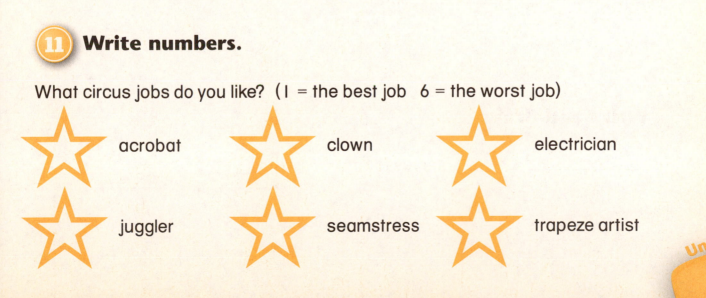

☆ acrobat   ☆ clown   ☆ electrician

☆ juggler   ☆ seamstress   ☆ trapeze artist

Review

12 **Complete the sentences. Use words from the box.**

| carpenter | journalist | plumber | teacher | waiter |

1. A _____ writes stories for newspapers.

2. A _____ builds things out of wood.

3. A _____ puts running water in our homes.

4. A _____ serves food.

5. A _____ helps us learn.

13 **Complete the sentences. Use words from the box.**

| cuts | fixes | helps | sells | teaches |

1. A barber _____ hair.

2. A dentist _____ teeth.

3. A salesperson _____ clothes.

4. A vet _____ sick animals.

5. A coach _____ sports.

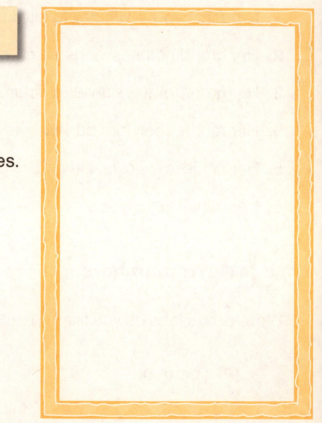

14 **Write and draw.**

A _____ serves food.
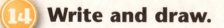

Cut-out Activity ✂ - - - - - - - - - - - - - - - -

A. **Cut out the cards. Match.**
B. **Find a partner.**
C. **Ask and answer questions about the helpers.**

ACROBATS	bring mail to people
ARCHITECTS	build things out of wood
CARPENTERS	design buildings
COACHES	fix teeth
DENTISTS	give us running hot and cold water
ELECTRICIANS	help sick animals
JOURNALISTS	help sick people
MAIL CARRIERS	put in electricity for lights, heat, and TV sets
NURSES	sell clothes or other things
PLUMBERS	serve food
SALESPEOPLE	sew clothes
TAILORS	teach sports
VETS	turn cartwheels
WAITERS	write stories for newspapers

Students cut out strips and match the helpers with their jobs. Students work with partners to ask and answer questions about the helpers. Students can also play a memory game with the cards.

3 Pen Pals

TRACK 09

1 **Listen and write. Use words from the boxes.**

Friends

Some of my friends live nearby,
   and some live far away—
   in France, Japan, and Paraguay.
I don't see them day to day.

We send each other e-mails,
   photos, and birthday cards.
I love to hear from all my friends.
It's fun and it isn't hard.

Friends with smiling faces,
   pen pals in distant places.
I've got friends I write to
   near and far.

I write about my _____ life
   and what I see each day—
   the crowded _____, the noisy _____,
   and parks where children play.

One pen pal lives in the country.
He writes me about the _____.
He feeds _____ in the yard
   and milks _____ in the _____.

(Chorus)

City	Country
cars	barn
city	chickens
streets	cows
	farm

2 **Write. Use words from the box.**

barns	buildings	cars	crops
fences	lakes	museums	restaurants

1. There are tall _____ in the city.

2. There are many _____ on the streets in the city.

3. There are _____ to visit in the city.

4. There are many noisy and busy _____ in the city.

5. There are houses with _____ around them in the country.

6. There are fields with _____ in the country.

7. There are big _____ in the country.

8. There are _____ for fishing in the country.

Grammar

| What does | he
she | **have to** do? | He
She | **has to** do homework. |
| What do | you
they | **have to** do? | I
They | **have to** do homework. |

3 **Write *has to* or *have to*.**

1. What does he have to do? He _____ clean his room.

2. What do they have to do? They _____ take the bus.

3. What does she have to do? She _____ go shopping.

4. What do you have to do? I _____ write to my pen pal.

5. What does she have to do? She _____ collect the eggs.

4 **Look at the chart. Then complete the sentences.
Use *has to* or *have to*.**

Anne	✔			
Lin	✔			
Pablo			✔	
Kim		✔		
Akiko				✔

1. Anne and Lin *have to do their homework.*

2. Pablo _____

3. Kim _____

4. Akiko _____

Make my bed. . .

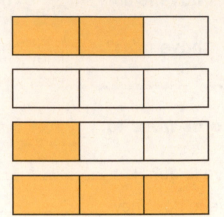

1. always

2. usually

3. sometimes

4. never

 Write sentences.

1. What do you always do in the morning?

   I always get dressed.

2. What do you usually do after school?

   _____

3. What do you sometimes do with your friend?

   _____

4. What do you do every day?

   _____

5. What do you never do in the morning?

   _____

7 Write questions.

1. _____

   I always eat breakfast.

2. _____

   She usually helps with the chores.

3. _____

   They sometimes go to the library.

Look. Complete the puzzle.

Across ➜

1. 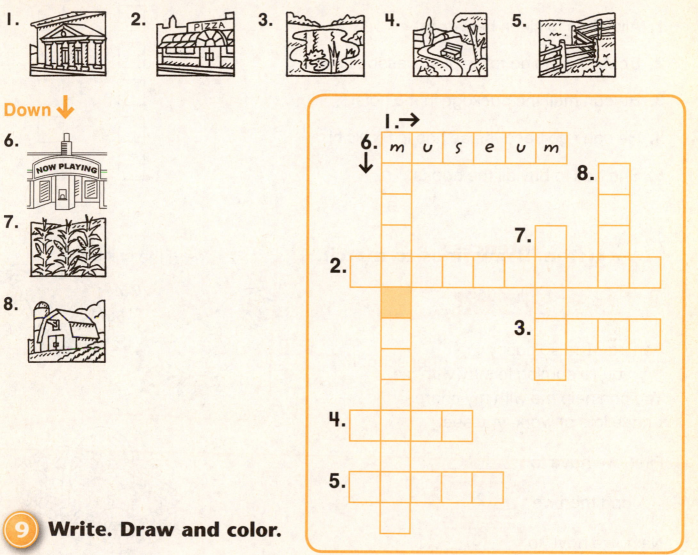   2.   3.   4.   5.

Down ↓

6.

7.

8.

1. ➜
6. ↓ | m | u | s | e | u | m |

8.

7.

2.

3.

4.

5.

⑨ **Write. Draw and color.**

Every day at school I have to _____

Unit 3

25

10 Listen. Check *yes* or *no*.

	Yes	No
1. Alice has to clean her room.	☐	☐
2. Bobby has to go to his piano lesson now.	☐	☐
3. He can mail the package in the hotel.	☐	☐
4. He can't go because he has to fix his bike.	☐	☐
5. She has to buy all the books.	☐	☐

11 Listen. Draw lines to match.

A Country Visit

Pen pal, I'm so happy
    you're coming to stay with me.
You can help me with my chores.
I have lots of work, you see.

First, we have to ___(1)___,

and then we ___(2)___.

Next, we have to ___(3)___.

I'll be glad to show you how.

But after work, we'll rest and play.
I promise you'll love your country stay!
And when I visit your home, too,
    I'll help you with all you have to do!

feed the chickens

collect the eggs

milk the cow

A City Visit

12 **Read *A City Visit*. Circle the words.**

1. Terry lives in _____.   Australia   Japan   China
2. Terry is flying to _____.   Japan   India   Korea
3. Masahiro is his _____.   sister   cousin   pen pal
4. Masahiro lives in _____.   the country   a house   an apartment
5. There are lots of _____ in Tokyo.   stores   farms   cows
6. Ueno Park has a _____.   farm   zoo   library

13 **Write about you.**

1. Where do you live?

_____

2. What interesting places are there to visit?

_____

3. What is your favorite place?

_____

14 **Complete the sentences.**

1

2

3

1. What does Mary usually have to do?

Mary _____

2. What does Paul have to do?

Paul _____

3. What do they always have to do?

They _____

4

5

6

4. What does Mario sometimes have to do?

He _____

5. What does Sue have to do?

She _____

6. What do they never have to do?

They _____

Cut-out Activity ✂ ---------------

A. **Choose, cut, and glue.**
B. **Check** *always, usually, sometimes,* **or** *never.*
C. **Find a partner.**
   Ask and answer.

What do you always do?

I always make my bed.

Activities	always	usually	sometimes	never

clean a barn	clean my room	feed a pet
get up at 6:00 A.M.	go shopping	go to bed early
make my bed	milk a cow	paint a fence
return books to the library	take a taxi	take music lessons
take the school bus	walk to school	write to a pen pal

Students glue activities they do and don't do. They check one of the columns for each activity. Then they work with a partner to ask and answer questions about how often they do things.

Unit 3

29

4 Amazing Animals

1 **Listen and write. Draw lines to match.**

Animals

Some of the animals live in the sea.
Whales swim under water,
　much faster than you and me.

Some of the animals fly in the air—
_____, _____,
　all kinds of birds.
How did they get there?

Animals live in all kinds of places
*　with all kinds of weather.*
Animals have all kinds of faces
*　with horns and teeth and feathers.*

Some of the animals live in ice and snow—
_____ and penguins.
They like it really cold.

Some of the animals live in desert sand.
Ducks, parrots, and _____ can't,
　but lizards and camels can.

(Chorus)

bats

jellyfish

eagles

polar bears

2 Write. Use words from the box.

desert	forest	ice and snow
ocean	plains	rain forest

1. Polar bears live in the

_____

2. Whales live in the

_____

3. Camels live in the

_____

4. Deer live in the

_____

5. Parrots live in the

_____

6. Zebras live on the

_____

| can | Can a parrot fly? | A parrot **can** fly. |
| can't | Can a parrot swim? | A parrot **can't** swim. |

3 **Write *can* or *can't*.**

I. A snake _____ fly.

2. A deer _____ climb a tree.

3. A shark _____ grow new teeth.

4. A camel _____ sweat.

5. An octopus _____ bite.

6. A kangaroo _____ walk backwards.

4 **Unscramble the questions. Write answers.**

I. ocean/the/giraffes/in/can/live

Can giraffes live in the ocean?

No, they can't.

2. the/camels/can/in/live/desert

_____

_____

3. live/the/in/polar bears/can/forest

_____

_____

4. snakes/live/can/trees/in

_____

_____

5 **What did you learn? Match. Then write sentences.**

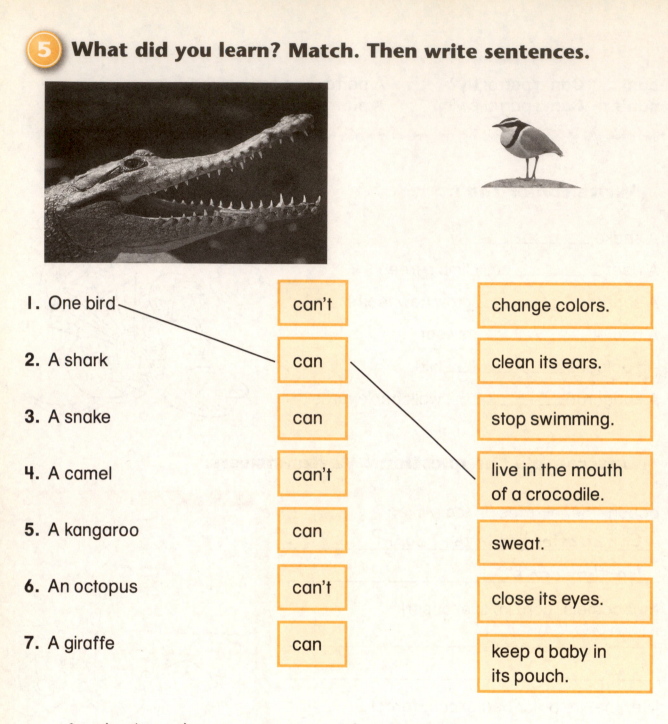

1. One bird —————— can't ————— change colors.

2. A shark ————————— can ———————— clean its ears.

3. A snake ———————— can ———————— stop swimming.

4. A camel ———————— can't ————— live in the mouth of a crocodile.

5. A kangaroo ———————— can ———————— sweat.

6. An octopus ———————— can't ————— close its eyes.

7. A giraffe ———————— can ———————— keep a baby in its pouch.

1. _One bird can live in the mouth of a crocodile._

2. _____

3. _____

4. _____

5. _____

6. _____

7. _____

6 **Write. Use words from the box.**

desert	ice	plains
rain forest	snow	

One day an animal said, "I need a place to live."

1. "I can't live in the ☐☐☐☐ and ☐☐☐ . Too cold!"

2. "I can't live in the ☐☐☐☐☐☐ . Too hot!"

3. "I can't live on the ☐☐☐☐☐☐ . Too much grass!"

4. "I can't live in the ☐☐☐☐ ☐☐☐☐☐☐ . Too many trees!"

Look at the letters in the yellow boxes. Write them in order.

Where can the animal live? It can live in the _____

7 **Write. Draw and color.**

This animal is _____ It lives _____

8 Listen. Complete the chart.

Animal	Where do they live?	What can they do?	What can't they do?
1. bats			
2. polar bears			
3. ostriches			
4. giraffes			
5. kangaroos			
6. camels			

9 Listen and write. Use words from the box.

If

If I could be an animal, a _____ is what I'd be.
I'd grow new teeth and skip the dentist.
That sounds great to me.

If I could be an animal, a _____ is what I'd be.
Formally dressed, I'd play in the snow.
That sounds fun to me.

If I could be an animal, a _____ is what I'd be.
I'd squeeze my dinner and eat for a week.
That sounds good to me.

If I could be an animal, a _____ is what I'd be.
I'd clean my ears without taking a bath.
That sounds cool to me.

giraffe
penguin
python
shark

Snake's Flying Lesson

10 **Read** *Snake's Flying Lesson.* **Write** *yes* **or** *no.*

1. Snake asks the birds to help.   <u>yes</u>
2. The birds help Snake to walk.   _____
3. Snake thinks flying is wonderful.   _____
4. Penguin says Snake is silly.   _____
5. Snake falls through the air.   _____

11 **Which animal do you want to be? Check one box.**
Write a sentence.

1.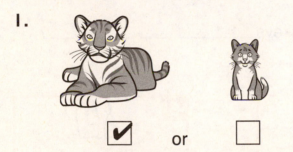
   ✔ **or** ☐

   <u>I want to be a tiger because</u>
   <u>tigers run fast.</u>

2.
   ☐ **or** ☐

   _____
   _____

3.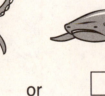
   ☐ **or** ☐

   _____
   _____

4.
   ☐ **or** ☐

Review

12 **Answer the questions. Circle *yes* or *no*.
Write sentences with *can* or *can't*.**

1. Can birds fly?   (Yes)   No   Birds _can fly._

2. Can camels live
   in the snow?   Yes   No   Camels _____

3. Can monkeys
   climb trees?   Yes   No   Monkeys _____

4. Can a whale live
   in the desert?   Yes   No   A whale _____

5. Can a shark grow
   new teeth?   Yes   No   A shark _____

6. Can a giraffe clean
   its own ears?   Yes   No   A giraffe _____

Cut-out Activity ✂----------------------

A. Cut out and glue the animal names in the chart above *can* or *can't*.

B. Choose and write what the animals can or can't do.

C. Find a partner. Ask and answer.

What can a bat do?

A bat can fly.

What can't a bat do?

A bat can't squirt ink.

can _____	can't _____	can _____
can't _____	can _____	can't _____
can _____	can't _____	can _____

A bat	A camel	A crocodile
A giraffe	A kangaroo	A monkey
An octopus	A shark	A snake

Animal Activities

run fast	squirt ink	live off fat in their bodies
reach high	grow new teeth often	live underground
change colors	clean own ears	sweat
jump	fly	squeeze other animals
walk backwards	close their eyes	go without water for a long time

Students complete the chart. They glue an animal name and write a phrase (from the box) that tells what the animal **can** or **can't** do. Students work with partners to ask and answer questions about the animals.

Unit 4

39

⑤ Rain or Shine

1 **Listen and write. Draw lines to match.**

Playing Outside

boots	coat
gloves	raincoat
sandals	sweater
swimsuit	

Hey, where's my _____?
It's a cool and windy day.
I need a cap and sweater
   to go outside and play.

Hey, where's my winter _____?
It's a cold and snowy day.
I need a coat, hat, and _____
   to go outside and play.

When the seasons change,
   the clothes I wear change, too.
No matter what the weather is,
   I play outside—don't you?

Hey, where's my _____?
It's a wet and rainy day.
I need a raincoat and some _____
   to go outside and play.

Hey, where's my _____?
It's a hot and sunny day.
I need my suit and _____
   to go outside and play.

(Chorus—repeat)

2 **Write. Use words from the box. Draw.**

cloudy	rainy	snowy
sunny	windy	

1.

Monday

2.

Tuesday

3.

Wednesday

1. Monday it was _____

2. Tuesday it was _____

3. Wednesday it was _____

4.

Thursday

5.

Friday

6.

Today

4. Thursday it was _____

5. Friday it was _____

6. Today it's _____

What **is** the weather like today?   Today it**'s** cool.
What **was** the weather like yesterday?   Yesterday it **was** windy.
Leaves **were** everywhere.

3 **Write *is* or *was*.**

1. Monday it _____ sunny.

2. Tuesday it _____ rainy.

3. Thursday it _____ cool.

4. Today it _____ hot.

5. Wednesday it _____ windy.

4 **Write *is* and *are* or *was* and *were*.**

the 1st   the 2nd   yesterday, the 3rd   today, the 4th

1. Today it _____ cloudy. There _____ clouds everywhere.

2. On the 2nd, it _____ rainy. There _____ puddles everywhere.

3. Yesterday it _____ windy. There _____ leaves everywhere.

4. On the 1st, it _____ sunny. There _____ people everywhere.

5 **Write about the weather.**

SATURDAY	SUNDAY	MONDAY	TUESDAY	TODAY

1. On Saturday, it _____
2. On Sunday, it _____
3. On Monday, it _____
4. On Tuesday, it _____
5. Today, it _____

Grammar

What do people **wear** in summer?

I We They	**wear** shorts and sandals.
He She	**wears** shorts and sandals.

6 **Write *wear* or *wears*.**

1. I _____ gloves in the winter.
2. She _____ boots when it's rainy.
3. They _____ sandals in the summer.
4. He _____ a sweater in the fall.
5. We _____ shorts when it's hot.

44

7 Look. Do the puzzle.

Across ➡

1. 2. 3. 4. 5. 6.

Down ⬇

7. 8. 9. 10. 11. 12.

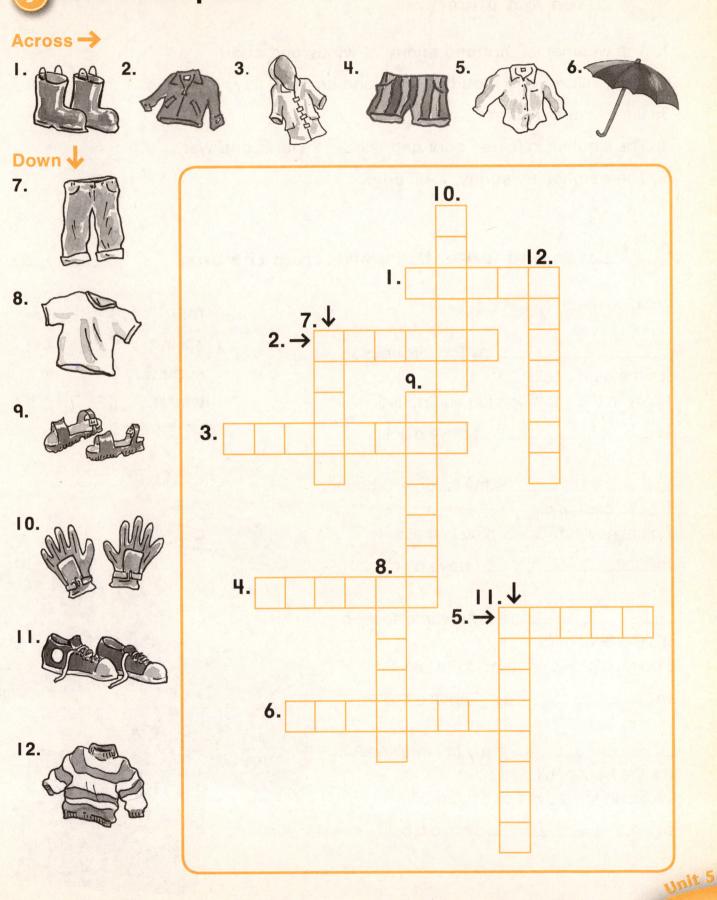

8 Listen and underline.

1. The weather is **hot and sunny. / windy and cool.**

2. It's a **warm and cloudy / cold and snowy** day.

3. It's a **rainy / windy** day.

4. The weather in fall is **cool and windy. / warm and wet.**

5. The weather is **sunny. / cloudy.**

9 Listen and write. Use words from the box.

Favorite Seasons

| fall |
| spring |
| summer |
| winter |

_____'s my favorite season.
It's the best of all.
I play in the snow or slide on my sled.
In _____, I have a ball!

_____ is my favorite season.
It's the best of all.
I plant new flowers or play in the park.
In _____, I have a ball!

_____'s my favorite season.
It's the best of all.
I go on a picnic or swim in the lake.
In _____, I have a ball!

_____ is my favorite season.
It's the best of all.
I jump in the leaves or ride my bike.
In _____, I have a ball!

A New Old Coat

10 **Read *A New Old Coat*. Circle.**

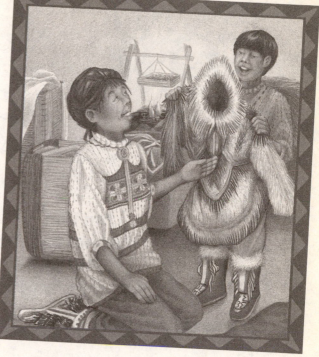

1. Meekitjuk is at his (winter) / summer house.

2. Meekitjuk's **sweater / coat** is too small.

3. Palluq says she can make a coat from a **box. / bag.**

4. Palluq gives Meekitjuk his **grandfather's / father's** coat.

5. Meekitjuk is **sad / happy** to have a new coat.

6. Meekitjuk will wear his new coat to play in the **snow. / rain.**

11 **What do you wear in the winter? Write a sentence. Draw.**

In the winter I wear _____

Review

12 **Write. Use words from the box.**

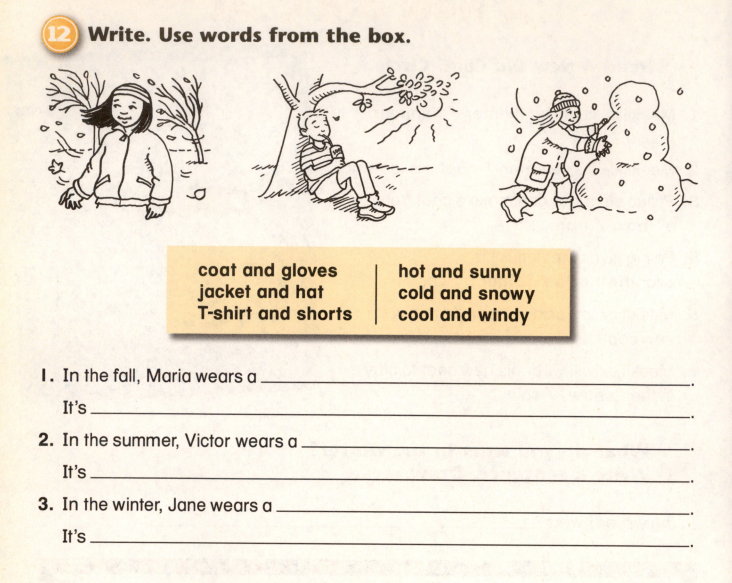

coat and gloves	hot and sunny
jacket and hat	cold and snowy
T-shirt and shorts	cool and windy

1. In the fall, Maria wears a _____.

It's _____.

2. In the summer, Victor wears a _____.

It's _____.

3. In the winter, Jane wears a _____.

It's _____.

13 **Write. Use words from the box.**

are
is
was
were

1. Yesterday it _____ rainy.

Puddles _____ everywhere.

2. Today it _____ cloudy.

Clouds _____ everywhere.

Cut-out Activity ✂

A. Cut out and glue the days of the week onto a sheet of paper. Start the week with Sunday.
B. What day is today? Write *Today* on that card.
C. What day was yesterday? Write *Yesterday* on that card.
D. Cut and glue a weather word to tell what the weather is like each day for one week. Draw the weather for each day.
E. Find a partner. Ask and answer questions.

What is the weather like today?

It's cool and windy.

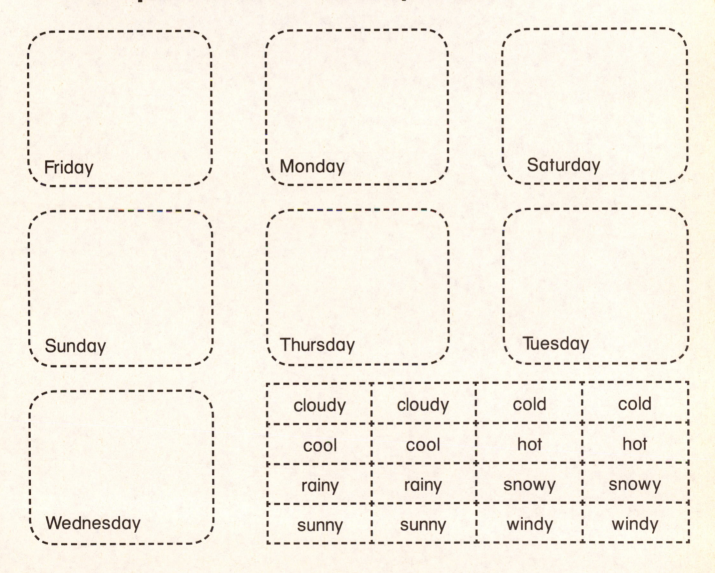

Friday	Monday	Saturday
Sunday	Thursday	Tuesday

Wednesday			
	cloudy	cloudy	cold	cold
	cool	cool	hot	hot
	rainy	rainy	snowy	snowy
	sunny	sunny	windy	windy

Students make weather calendars for one week. They ask and answer questions about the weather.

Unit 5

49

6 Our Five Senses

1 Listen and write. Use words from the box. Draw lines to match.

hear	smell
see	touch

Street Fair

At the street fair I can _____
    so many things to buy—
jewelry, clothes, toys, and pets,
    and books piled up high.

At the street fair I can _____
    delicious food to eat.
I can taste the popcorn
    and the ice cream cones so sweet.

*At the street fair, at the street fair—
    my senses come alive.
At the street fair, at the street fair—
    one, two, three, four, five.*

At the street fair I can _____
    laughter from the crowd.
A little monkey with a drum
    and sticks is playing loud.

At the street fair I can look at
    things both old and new.
I love to look and _____ them all,
    then buy just one or two.

(Chorus)

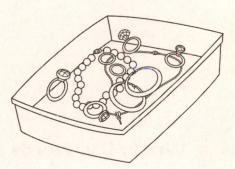

2 **Look and write. Use words from the box.**

ear	eye	finger
nose	tongue	

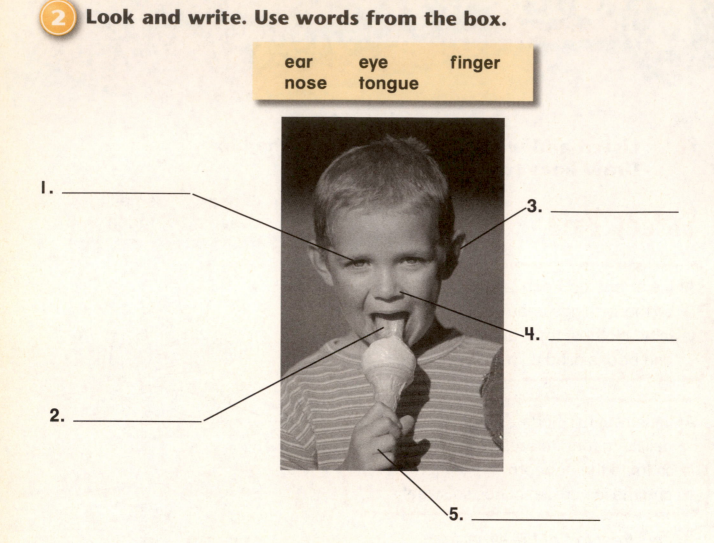

1. _____

2. _____

3. _____

4. _____

5. _____

3 **Write. Use words from the box.**

hear	see	smell
taste	touch	

1. I _____ with my eyes.

2. I _____ with my ears.

3. I _____ with my tongue.

4. I _____ with my fingers.

5. I _____ with my nose.

52

4 **Read and write.**

1. How do the flowers look?

   They _____ pretty.

2. How do the sirens sound?

   They _____ loud.

3. How does the rabbit feel?

   It _____ soft.

4. How does the paint smell?

   It _____ strong.

5. How does the ice cream taste?

   It _____ sweet.

5 **Write. Use words from the box.**

| feel   look   sound |

1. The music

   _____ bad.

2. The rock

   _____ rough.

3. Her clothes

   _____ dirty.

The drum **was** loud.   The kittens **were** so soft.

6 **Write _was_ or _were_.**

Yesterday wasn't a good day.

1. The milk _____ bad.

2. The babies _____ loud.

3. There _____ sticky glue on my book.

4. The TV _____ very loud.

5. The shoes _____ too small. Ouch!

7 **Complete the sentences.**

1. Why do you like watermelon?

   Because it _____.

2. Why do you like flowers?

   Because they _____.

3. Why do you like rabbits?

   Because they _____.

4. Why do you like popcorn?

   Because it _____.

8 Do the puzzle. Use words from the box.

| bad | fresh | heavy | loud | sharp |
| smooth | sour | sticky | strong | sweet |

Across →

1. the lemon tastes _____
2. the pin point feels _____
3. the glass feels _____
4. the medicine tastes _____
5. the glue feels _____

Down ↓

6. the music sounds _____
7. the candy tastes _____
8. the suitcase looks _____
9. the soap smells _____
10. the paint smells _____

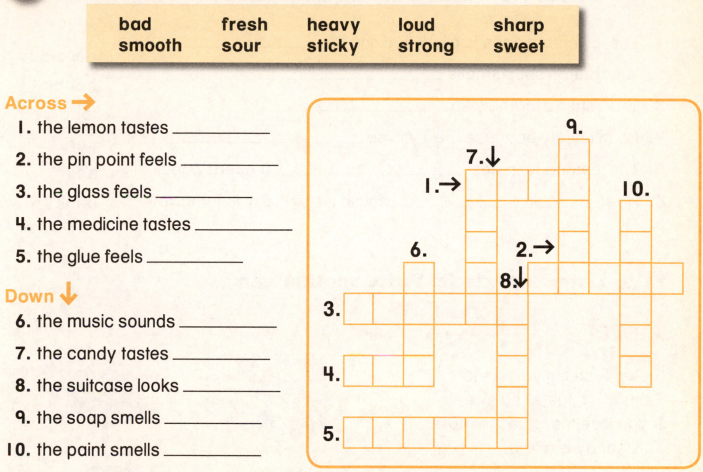

9 Read. What is it? Draw and color.

It feels wet. It smells and tastes salty. It looks blue and beautiful.
It sounds soft. People go there on hot and sunny days.

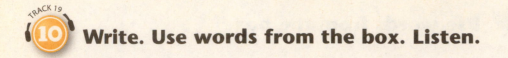

TRACK 19

10 **Write. Use words from the box. Listen.**

1. The ice cream cone is all melted and _____.

2. Your mom's soup smells _____.

3. Your kitten's fur feels so _____.

4. I can't study because the TV is so _____.

5. The lemonade tastes _____. It needs sugar.

6. He's _____ because his birthday is tomorrow.

delicious
happy
loud
soft
sour
sticky

TRACK 20

11 **Listen and circle. Write another verse.**

More!

Sister, Sister, give me more.
This ____ tastes so sweet.
If you love me, give me more.
This candy is a treat!

Mama, Mama, give me more.
That ____ smells so good.
If you love me, give me more.
Thanks. I knew you would!

Daddy, Daddy, give me more.
My ____ feels so light.
If you love me, give me more.
More coins will make it right!

★ ★ ★ ★ ★

_____, _____, give me more.

That _____ looks so good.
If you love me, give me more.
Thanks. I knew you would!

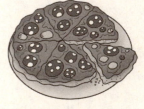

Dora the Detective

12 **Read *Dora the Detective*. Write. Use words from the box.**

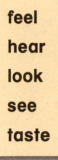

feel
hear
look
see
taste

Dora likes to play detective. She finds some tracks. In her house, she

_____ a big, empty box. Dora eats a cracker. It _____

bad. Then, she _____ a strange noise. In the other room, she

sees a parrot. The parrot _____ beautiful. Polly's feathers

_____ soft.

13 **What happens next? Write. Draw.**

Then Dora gives Polly a

_____.

"Oh!" says Polly. "It tastes

_____!"

Review

14 **Write. Use words from the box.**

_____   _____   _____   _____

15 **Complete the sentences. Use words from the boxes.**

1. The lemons _____ sour.
2. The sky _____ beautiful.
3. The music _____ wonderful.
4. The rabbits _____ soft.
5. The flowers _____ sweet.

> feel
> looks
> smell
> sounds
> taste

6. The chips taste _____
7. The kitten looks _____
8. The fire truck sounds _____
9. The sandpaper feels _____
10. The perfume smells _____

> loud
> rough
> salty
> soft
> sweet

Cut-out Activity ✂

A. **Draw and color.**
B. **Cut out the cards.**
C. **Find a partner.**
   Ask and answer questions.

How does a rabbit feel?

It feels soft.

How do the boys look?

They look happy.

feel hard	feel sharp	feels soft	look beautiful	look happy
looks tired	smells delicious	smells fresh and clean	smells strong	smells sweet
sound pretty	sounds loud	taste bad	tastes salty	tastes sweet

Students draw and color appropriate things on each card. Students may glue or arrange the cards on a sheet or paper for a game board. They can use a game marker and ask and answer questions about what's on the squares they land on.

Unit 6

59

7 A World of Food

 TRACK 21

1 **Listen. Draw the food.**

Food, Glorious Food

In the morning, in the afternoon,
eating food is great.
Breakfast, lunch, or dinner—
I can hardly wait.
What do you have on your plate?

For breakfast, I'll have
some toast and jam
some milk and cereal,
some bread and ham.

At lunch time, I'm going to have
some soup,
a healthful salad,
and then some fruit.

(Chorus)

For dinner, I'll have
some fish and rice.
And for dessert,
perhaps cake would be nice.

Or maybe I'll have
onions and peas,
chicken and vegetables,
lettuce and cheese.

(Chorus)

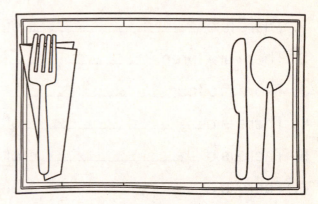

breakfast

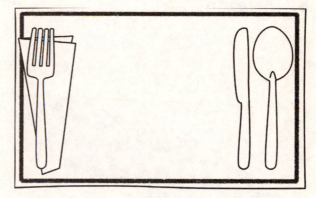

lunch

dinner

2 Write. Use words from the box.

bottle	bowl	bunch	cans
jar	loaf	pieces	slices

1. There is a _____ of oil.

2. There are three _____ of cheese.

3. There are four _____ of soda.

4. There is a _____ of pickles.

5. There is a _____ of olives.

6. There is a _____ of grapes.

7. There are two _____ of tomato.

8. There is a _____ of bread.

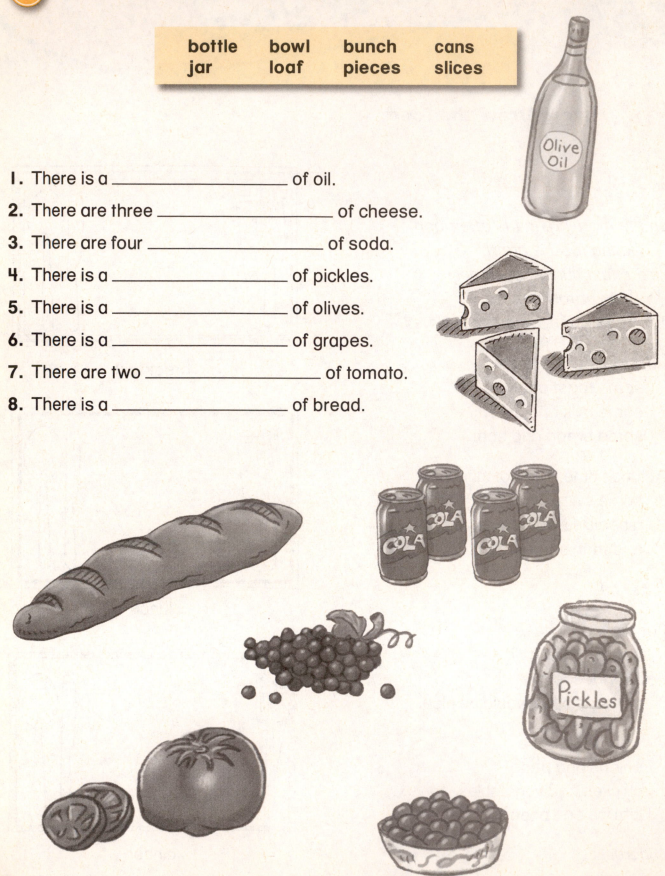

Are there **any** pickles on the table?   Yes, there are two jars of pickles.
Are there **any** grapes on the table?   Yes, there is one bunch of grapes.
Are there **any** bananas on the table?   No, there aren't **any**.

3 **Look and write.**

1. Are there any lemons on the table?

_____

2. Are there any carrots?

_____

3. Are there any cherries?

_____

4. Are there any oranges?

_____

5. Are there any apples?

_____

6. Are there any olives?

_____

7. Are there any peppers?

_____

8. Are there any tomatoes?

_____

| Is there | Is there any milk? | Yes, **there's** some milk.
There's one bottle of milk.
No, **there isn't** any milk. |
| Are there | Are there any cookies? | Yes, **there are** some cookies.
There are two bags of cookies.
No, **there aren't** any cookies. |

4 **Write sentences. Use the words.**

1. Is there any rice?

   _____ (some)

   _____ (box)

   _____ (No)

2. Are there any pickles?

   _____ (some)

   _____ (jars)

   _____ (No)

5 **Write questions.**

1. _____

   There are two cans of peas.

2. _____

   Yes, there's some fruit juice.

3. _____

   No, there aren't any mangoes.

6 Find the food words. Use the pictures as clues. Circle.

```
e  g  g  r  g  r  a  p  e  s
l  t  o  m  a  t  o  w  b  c
m  e  g  t  b  p  c  d  r  h
i  d (c  h  e  e  s  e) e  i
l  o  a  l  i  a  e  j  a  c
k  f  r  j  t  r  k  p  d  k
e  i  r  p  e  p  p  e  r  e
a  s  o  f  u  m  n  s  a  n
j  h  t  b  a  n  a  n  a  i
s  e  s  e  o  n  i  o  n  m  b
```

7 Write about you.

1. What do you eat for breakfast?

   I eat _____.

2. What do you eat for lunch?

   I eat _____.

3. What do you eat for dinner?

   I eat _____.

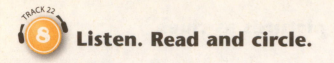 **Listen. Read and circle.**

TRACK 22

1. Which dinner is delicious?

2. The fruit salad doesn't have any.

3. The spaghetti sauce doesn't have any.

4. Which foods come from Asia?

5. What's for dessert?

TRACK 23

9 **Listen. Read and write. Color.**

Desserts

Pour some chocolate syrup
    on top of your ice cream.

Put on a bright red _____.
This dessert's a dream!

Take two chocolate _____.
Put peanut butter on one.
Put the other cookie on top.
Cookie sandwiches are fun!

Ice cream, pie, and cookies.

I love a good _____.
But never eat them all at once,
    or your tummy will really hurt!

Delicious Snacks

10 **Read *Delicious Snacks*. How do you make this delicious snack? Write numbers.**

( ) Put on some cream cheese.

( ) Cut each stalk into three pieces.

(1) Wash the celery stalks.

( ) Eat and enjoy.

( ) Take off the leaves.

( ) Put raisins on top.

11 **Write. Draw.**

What's your favorite snack?

My favorite snack is _____

What is in your favorite snack?

It has _____

Review

12 **Read and circle.**

1. olives

2. cherries

3. bread

4. lamb chops

13 **Write. Use words from the box.**

1. a _____ of juice
2. a _____ of cheese
3. a _____ of grapes
4. a _____ of soda
5. a _____ of apples
6. a _____ of pickles
7. a _____ of chicken
8. a _____ of rice

bottle
bowl
box
bunch
can
jar
piece
plate

Cut-out Activity ✂

A. **Draw the foods.**
B. **Cut out the cards.**
   Put them in a pile.
C. **Find a partner.**
   Ask and answer.

Are there any apples?

Yes, there are some apples.

Is there any milk?

No, there isn't any.

My Favorite Foods

---

apples	banana	bottle of water	bowl of cherries	box of rice
bunch of grapes	carrot	celery	corn	fish
four cookies	ice cream	jar of pickles	loaf of bread	pear
pieces of cheese	sandwich	slices of tomato	three potatoes	two cans of soda

Students draw a picture using 5–10 food items from the cards. Then they cut out the cards and place them in a pile. Students work with partners to draw cards from the pile and ask about the food shown in each other's pictures.

Unit 7

69

8 In Shape!

best
bike
cake
great
health
hike
rest
yourself

1 Write words from the box. Then listen to check.

Feeling Good

I eat lots of fruit and vegetables,
    but not much pie or _____.
I drink lots of water and some juice
    to keep me feeling _____.

Outside, I get plenty of exercise,
I skate and ride my _____.
I play some soccer with my friends,
    and sometimes, I take a
    _____.

I make sure when I'm at home
    to look and feel my _____.
I take a shower, brush my teeth,
    and then get lots of _____.

'Cause I'm in shape and feeling good.
I know the rules for _____.
Do like me, and you will learn
    to take care of _____!

(Chorus)

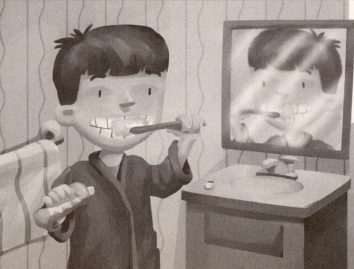

Write. Use words from the box.

Do and Don't

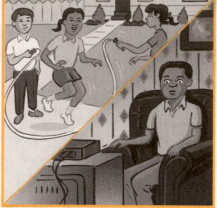

1. _____ enough good food.
2. _____ too much. (negative)
3. _____ enough exercise.
4. _____ too much TV. (negative)
5. _____ enough sleep.
6. _____ too late. (negative)

eat
get
stay up
watch

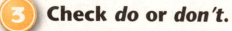 **Check *do* or *don't*.**

	Do	Don't
1. Brush your teeth every day.	☐	☐
2. Eat a lot of chocolate.	☐	☐
3. Take a bath or shower every day.	☐	☐
4. Stay inside all day.	☐	☐
5. Ride in a car everywhere.	☐	☐

Did you **get** enough exercise yesterday?   Yes, I **did**.   No, I **didn't**.
Did Billy **get** enough exercise yesterday?   Yes, he **did**.   No, he **didn't**.
Did Laura **get** enough exercise yesterday?   Yes, she **did**.   No, she **didn't**.
Did Ken and Pat **get** enough exercise yesterday?   Yes, they **did**.   No, they **didn't**.

4 **Write.**

didn't = did not

1. Did he get enough exercise yesterday? Yes, _he did._____

2. Did she eat fruit and vegetables? Yes, _____

3. Did they drink enough water? No, _____

4. Did she eat enough good food? Yes, _____

5. Did he get enough sleep? No, _____

6. Did you drink soda yesterday? No, _____

5 **Look. Write about you.**

1. Did you brush your teeth yesterday? _____

2. Did you get enough sleep? _____

3. Did you drink plenty of water? _____

4. Did you eat fruit and vegetables? _____

Did you **get** enough sleep?   Yes, I **got** nine hours of sleep.
Did you **eat** enough vegetables?   Yes, I **ate** a lot of vegetables.
Did you **drink** enough water?   Yes, I **drank** eight glasses of water.

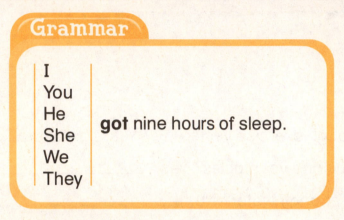

Grammar

I	
You	
He	
She	**got** nine hours of sleep.
We	
They	

6 **Write. Use *got, ate,* or *drank*.**

1. Sandy _____ plenty of sleep.

2. Alan _____ lots of water and juice.

3. Sue and Dan _____ too much candy.

4. Teresa _____ fruit and vegetables.

5. I _____ too much soda yesterday.

6. Sylvia _____ plenty of exercise.

7 **Read and write.**

Did you get enough exercise yesterday?

Yes, _____
_____

Did you eat enough good food yesterday?

Yes, _____
_____

8 Complete the questions. Use *did* and a word from the box.

1. _____ you _____ enough sleep yesterday?
2. _____ he _____ fruit and vegetables?
3. _____ they _____ plenty of water?
4. _____ she _____ enough exercise?
5. _____ you _____ your teeth yesterday?
6. _____ he _____ a bath or shower?

brush
drink
eat
get
take

9 Complete the sentences. Use the words to do the puzzle.

candy	drink	enough	exercise
health	sleep	soda	

1. _____ plenty of water every day.
2. Eat _____ vegetables every day.
3. Don't drink too much _____.
4. _____ rules are very important.
5. Don't eat too much _____.
6. _____ eight hours every night.
7. Get enough _____.
8. Get _____!

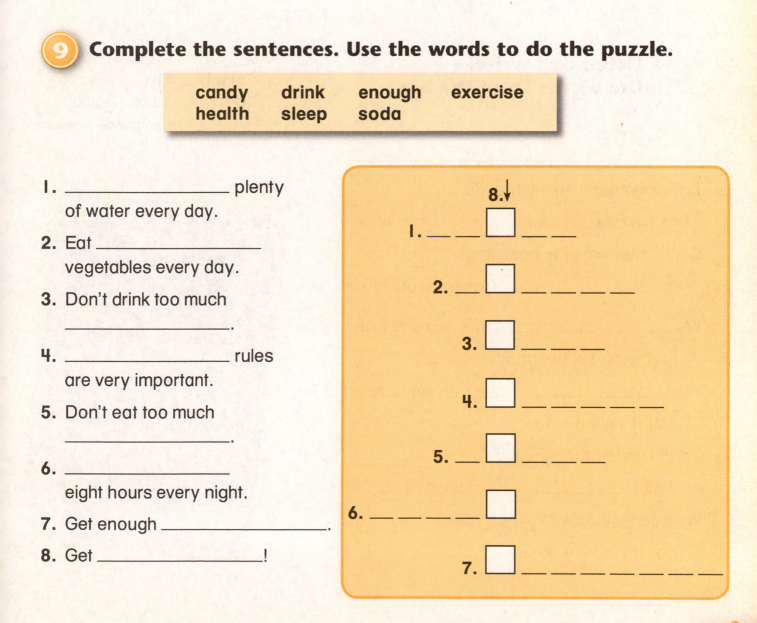

10 Listen. Read and circle.

1. That piece is so big. Don't _____. **a.** try to move it **b.** eat too much

2. I ate all my _____. **a.** broccoli **b.** asparagus

3. It's a great day. Let's _____. **a.** go shopping **b.** go swimming

4. You always _____. **a.** get enough sleep **b.** get enough exercise

5. Did she drink soda? **a.** No, she didn't. She drank water. **b.** Yes, she did. She drank two cans.

6. Don't _____. **a.** stay up too late **b.** forget to exercise

11 Listen and write. Use words from the box.

climb	fly	have
play	take	stay

Outside

I get together with my friends

to swim or _____ our kites.

Sometimes we play basketball

or _____ races on our bikes.

We _____ some fruit and water

for a picnic in the park.

We _____ and run and have great fun

until it's almost dark.

I don't understand the kids

who _____ inside all day.

Who cares about TV when you

can go outside to _____?

Exercise Is Fun!

12 **Read _Exercise Is Fun!_ Match. Write the letter.**

ⓐ

ⓑ

ⓒ

ⓓ

ⓔ

ⓕ

_e_ **1.** Boris is climbing a rock wall.

____ **2.** Asma is practicing ballet.

____ **3.** Justin is riding a horse.

____ **4.** David is practicing karate.

____ **5.** Flor is doing yoga.

____ **6.** Anita is jumping on a trampoline.

13 **How do you get exercise? Check. Draw one way you exercise.**

☐ climb

☐ dance

☐ do gymnastics

☐ do karate

☐ do yoga

☐ jump

☐ play baseball

☐ play soccer

☐ play volleyball

☐ ride a bike

☐ run

☐ swim

Review

14 **Read and look. Complete the sentences.**

1. Eat enough good food. Eat  and _____ .

   _____   _____

   Don't eat too much _____ or drink too much _____ .

   _____   _____

2. Get enough exercise. Ride a _____ or play _____ .

   _____   _____

   Don't watch too much _____ or _____ too much.

   _____   _____

15 **Complete the sentences. Use *ate*, *drank*, and *got*.**

1. Yesterday Paul _____ good food and _____ lots of water.
2. He _____ enough exercise and _____ enough sleep.

16 **Write. Are you in shape? Why or why not?**

_____

_____

_____

78

Cut-out Activity ✂ - - - - - - - - - - - - - -

A. **Cut out the cards.**
B. **Find a partner.**
   Ask and answer
   questions.

Did you eat enough
fruit yesterday?

Yes, I did.

Did you drink enough
water yesterday?

No, I didn't.

drink juice	drink milk	drink water	eat fruit
eat vegetables	get exercise	get fresh air	get sleep

Students cut out the cards. They work with partners and ask and answer questions about
each other's habits. Students can also draw examples on the back of the cards and ask
and answer *What did you eat/drink?*, etc.

9 Puppets

1 **Choose six words from the box and write. Then listen.**

cartoon	finger	friends	puppet	sandwich
shadow	show	sticks	story	strings

Puppets for Sale

Do you want someone to play with?
Do you have an idea for a show?

I'm a _____ and I'll be your friend.
I'm ready to play—let's go!

You can make a puppet, any size,

   with paper bags, _____, and things.
From a simple sock with a pair of eyes,
   to a marionette with strings.

Some are thumb and _____ puppets.
You can wear them on your hand.

_____ puppets need a bright light
   to do their shadow dance.

Do you want to tell a _____
   in a new, exciting way?
We are puppets and we'll be your _____.
We're ready to go—let's play!

Do you like puppets?

2 **Write. Use words from the box. Read and look.**

boring	exciting	funny	scary

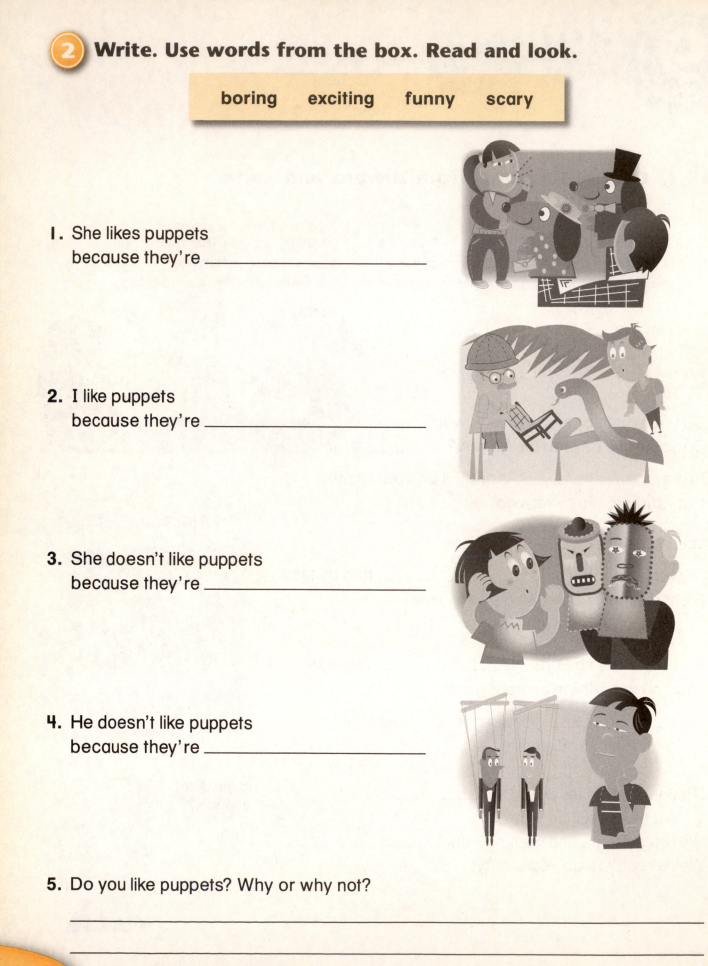

1. She likes puppets
   because they're _____

2. I like puppets
   because they're _____

3. She doesn't like puppets
   because they're _____

4. He doesn't like puppets
   because they're _____

5. Do you like puppets? Why or why not?

   _____

   _____

What **did** you **see**? I **saw** *Punch and Judy*.
What **did** he **see**? He **saw** *The Three Little Pigs*.
What **did** they **see**? They **saw** *The Bone Man*.

3 **Write.**

1. She _____ a puppet show.

2. He _____ a cartoon.

3. They _____ the movie.

4. I _____ a game.

4 **Write questions.**

1. What _____ she _____?
   She saw *Flim, Flam, and Flopsy*.

2. What _____ he _____?
   He saw *Punch and Judy*.

3. What _____ you _____?
   I saw *Flim, Flam, and Flopsy*.

Flim, Flam, and Flopsy

Don't miss
PUNCH & JUDY
****
TODAY
12:00 Noon

Punch & Judy

Did you **like** the show? Yes, I **liked** the show. No, I **didn't like** it.
Did she **like** the show? Yes, she **liked** it. No, she **didn't like** it.
Did they **like** the show? Yes, they **liked** it. No, they **didn't like** it.

5 **Write.**

1. She _____ the show.

2. He _____ the cartoon.

3. I _____ the movie.

4. They _____ the parade.

6 **Read and look. Choose. Write.**

a cartoon	didn't like	was boring
a puppet show	liked	was exciting
a soccer game	saw	was funny

1. What did they see? They _____

2. Did they like it? Yes, they _____

3. Why? Because _____

4. What did she see? She _____

5. Did she like it? No, she _____

6. Why? Because _____

7 **Find the words. Use the pictures as clues. Circle.**

x	r	q	w	s	j	r	y	p	o
c	w	q	v	p	b	l	x	x	z
v	i	d	e	o	g	a	m	e	s
p	m	i	r	r	c	z	o	w	f
m	u	v	c	t	e	w	v	q	x
v	c	r	z	s	w	q	i	x	u
z	q	w	r	h	g	c	e	r	q
c	a	r	t	o	o	n	s	q	z

8 **What do you like? Why? Write.**

I like _____

_____

_____

_____

Talk with a partner.

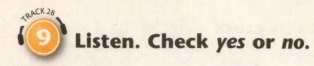

TRACK 28

9 **Listen. Check *yes* or *no*.**

	Yes	No
1. *Attack of the Giant Scorpions* was scary.	☐	☐
2. She thinks puppets are funny.	☐	☐
3. They think video games are exciting.	☐	☐
4. They think cartoons are boring.	☐	☐
5. The school puppet show was bad.	☐	☐

TRACK 29

10 **Listen and write. Use words from the box. Draw and color.**

Puppet Play

cry	decide	have	make
move	play	throw	use

When you _____ with puppets,

    you're the puppeteer.

You _____ what they will do—

    run or clap or cheer.

You can _____ their costumes,

    and decide what they will say.

Use your hand or strings to make

    them _____ a certain way.

You can paint their faces,

    and make them laugh or _____.

You can have them fight with swords

    or even _____ a pie!

Your puppets are your actors

    to _____ in your own play.

With your own imagination,

    you'll _____ fun all day!

Finish me!

Puppets Around the World

11 **Read *Puppets Around the World*. Match. Write the letter. Draw a line to the picture.**

1. Marionettes _____

2. Shadow puppets _____

3. Rod puppets _____

4. Water puppets _____

a. have light behind them.

b. look like they are standing on water.

c. are puppets with strings.

d. are moved with sticks.

12 **What puppet do you like the best? Why? Write.**

I like _____ because _____

_____

Review

 Complete the sentences. Use *funny, boring, scary,* or *exciting.*

1. She thinks it's _____

2. He thinks it's _____

3. Maria thinks it's _____

4. Tom thinks it's _____

14 Look. Complete the sentences.

1. What did they see? They _____

2. Did they like it? No, _____

3. Why? Because _____

4. What did she see? She _____

5. Did she like it? Yes, _____

6. Why? Because _____

Cut-out Activity ✂ - - - - - - - - - - - - - - - -

A. Cut out the cards and glue.
B. Find a partner. Ask and answer questions. Use words from the box or your own words.
C. Check and write your partner's answers.

What did you see?

I saw a water puppet show.

Did you like it? Why?

Yes, I did. Because the puppets were funny.

boring	exciting
funny	scary

What did you see?	Did you like it? Yes No	Why?

baseball game	cartoon	circus
game show	marionette show	movie
rod puppet show	shadow puppet show	soccer game
tennis game	TV show	water puppet show

Students glue seven strips on the chart or write their own ideas. After asking a partner the question in the first column, they check *yes* or *no* and then write *why* using one of the words from the word box or their own words.

1 Say the words. How many times do you hear **u** as in **ru**ler?

community   computer   costume   glue   January   juice   July   tofu

2 Do the crossword puzzle. Write words with the same sound as the **u** in **ru**ler.

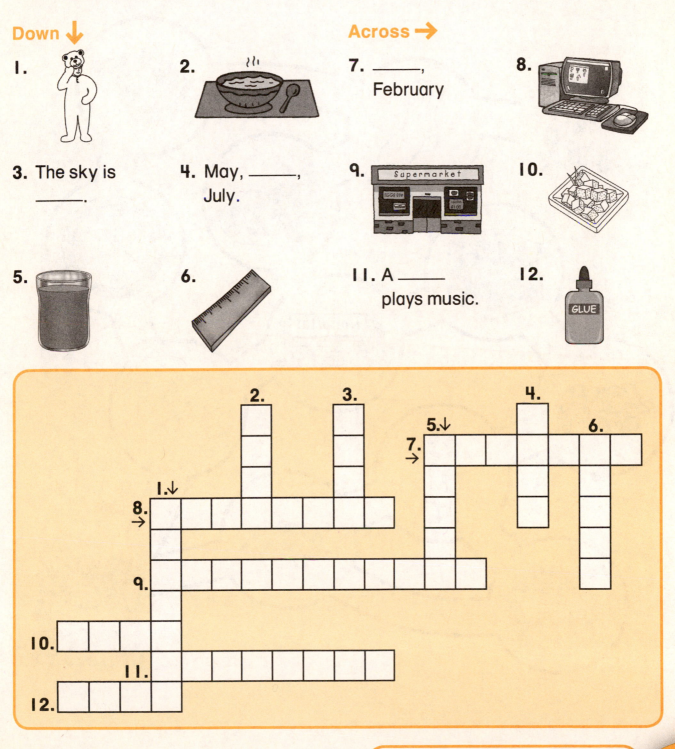

Down ↓

1.

2.

3. The sky is _____.

4. May, _____, July.

5.

6.

Across →

7. _____, February

8.

9.

10.

11. A _____ plays music.

12.

1 **Say the words. How many times do you hear *o* as in *dog*?**

box   clock   doctor   hopscotch   hospital   not   sock   stop

2 **Help Bob find his baseball. Find the path using words with the same sound as the *o* in *dog*.**

Start

End

1 Say the words. How many times do you hear **w** as in **w**orm?

sandwich   shower   towel   twenty   water   window   worm

2 Draw an X over the word that doesn't have the same sound as the **w** in **w**orm.

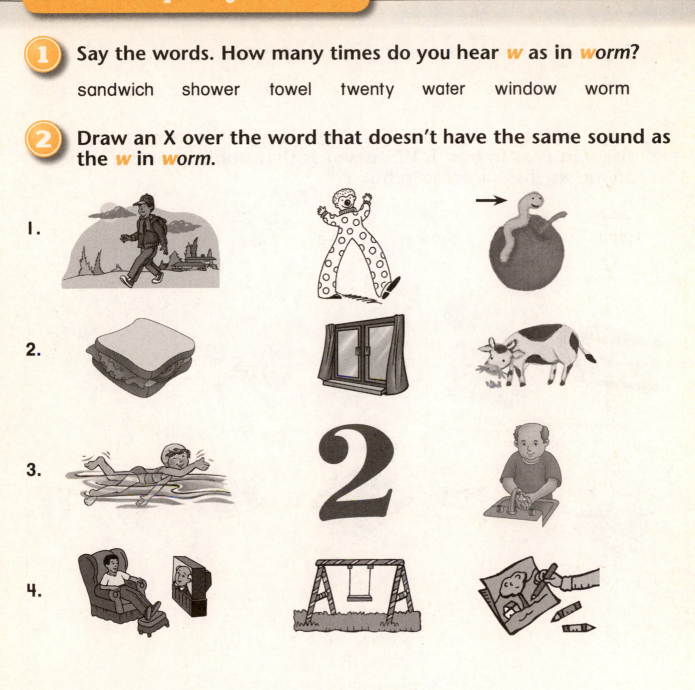

1.

2.

3.

4.

3 Look at 2. Write the words with the same sound as the **w** in **w**orm.

_____   _____   _____   _____

_____   _____   _____

1 Say the words. How many times do you hear *a* as in c*a*ke?

baby   baseball   eraser   Friday   game   name   paper   potato

2 Look at the pictures. Write the words with the same sound as the *a* in c*a*ke in box 1. Write words that don't have the same sound as the *a* in c*a*ke in box 2.

baby   ball   cake   game   grapes
plane   shadow   skates   sneaker   table

❶

❷

① **Say the words. How many times do you hear *e* as in z*e*bra?**

cheese   coffee   cookie   eat   evening   feed   he   zebra

② **Unscramble and write eight words with the same sound as the *e* in z*e*bra. Draw lines to match.**

ocekio   rete   lepse   rodbemo   bearz
cei mrcae   bertorh   kemony   ehsece   yffit

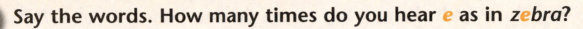

1. _____

2. _____

50

3. _____

4. _____

5. _____

6. _____

7. _____

8. _____

1 Say the words. How many times do you hear **o** as in *sofa*?

boat   cold   home   nose   potato   soap   stove   yellow

2 Find nine pictures of words with the same sound as the **o** in *sofa*. Color the pictures.

3 Look at 2. Write nine words with the same sound as the **o** in *sofa*.

_____   _____   _____

_____   _____   _____

_____   _____   _____

1 **Say the words. How many times do you hear *sh* as in *sh*oe?**

bush   fish   mushroom   shadow   sharp   shelf   short   wash

2 **Look and write the sentences. Say the sentences.**

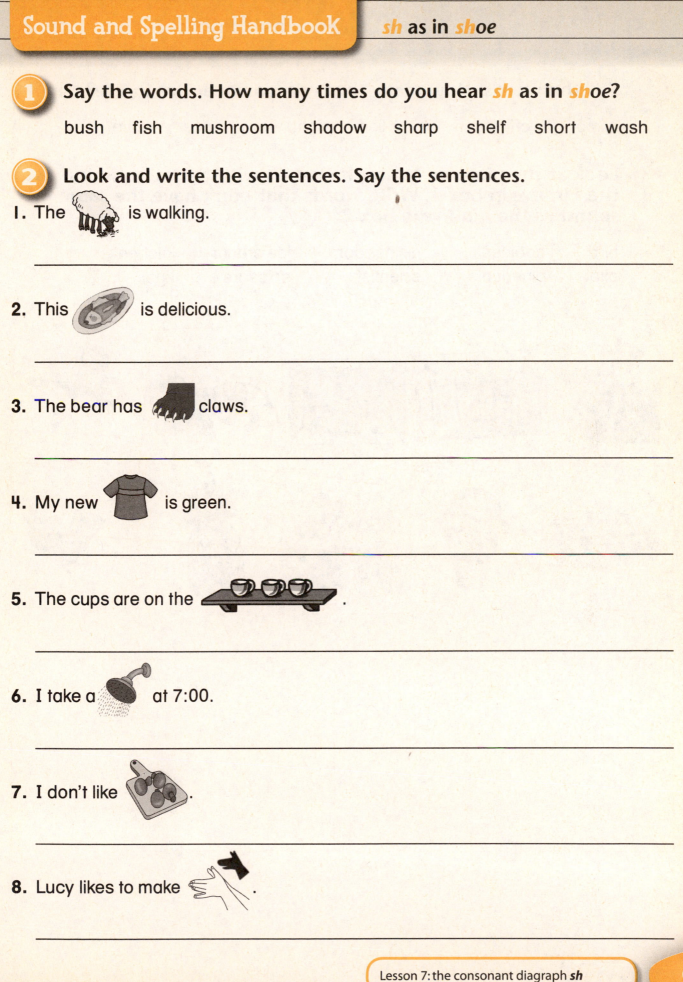

1. The   is walking.

_____

2. This   is delicious.

_____

3. The bear has   claws.

_____

4. My new   is green.

_____

5. The cups are on the   .

_____

6. I take a   at 7:00.

_____

7. I don't like   .

_____

8. Lucy likes to make   .

_____

1 Say the words. How many times do you hear **i** as in **five**?

climb   firefighter   kite   lion   night   pie   rice   white

2 Look at the pictures. Write the words with the same sound as the **i** in **five** in box 1. Write words that don't have the same sound as the **i** in **five** in box 2.

bird   cookies   dining room   ice cream   kitchen
pilot   pineapple   scientist   scissors   tiger

1

2

1 **Say the words. How many times do you hear *ch* as in *chair*?**

catch   chalk   cheetah   chicken   chocolate   lunch   touch   watch

2 **Charlie wants to eat cheese pizza. Find the path using words with the same sound as the *ch* in *chair*.**

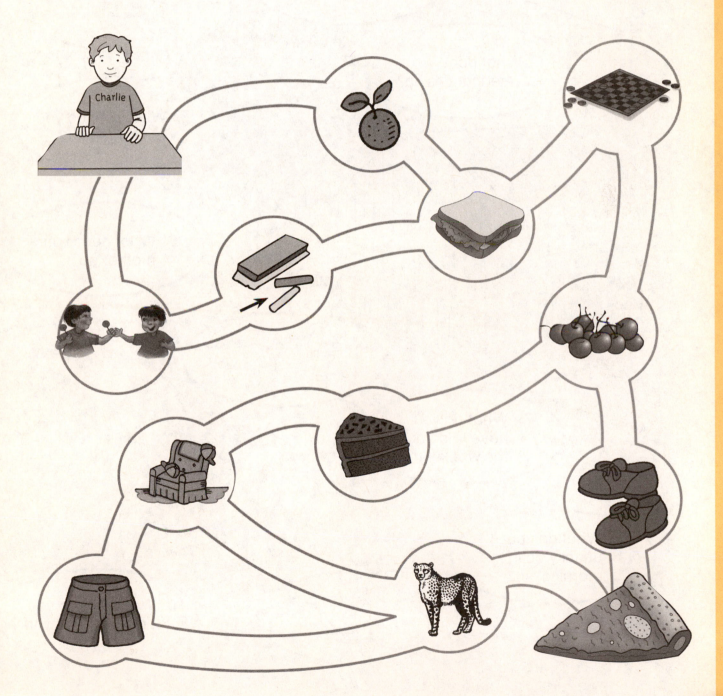

Move your game piece. Ask and answer.

START

1. What do veterinarians do?

2. What do you do after school?

3.

4. What time do you eat breakfast?

5. What does your mother do?

6.

7. What do you have to do on the weekend?

8. What do you usually do in the morning?

9.

10. What time do you do your homework?

Move your game piece. Ask and answer.

START

1. How do lemons taste?

2. Where do ostriches live?

3.

4. What can giraffes do?

5. What do you wear in the winter?

6.

7. What's the weather like in summer?

8. Describe sandpaper.

9.

10. Where do penguins live?

11. What can sharks do?

How do lemons taste?

They taste sour.

16. How do fire trucks sound?

17. Describe your favorite animal.

15.

18.

14. What's the weather like in fall?

19. How do kittens feel?

13. What do you wear in the summer?

20. What do you wear in the spring?

12.

21.

FINISH

Students move game pieces and answer the questions or describe or identify the images. Students only move ahead if they answer the question correctly. The first person to reach "Finish," wins.

Move your game piece. Ask and answer.

START

1. What's in your refrigerator?

2. Are there any carrots in your refrigerator?

3.

4. Did you get enough sleep last night?

5. What did you eat this morning?

6.

7. What movie did you see this month?

8. Did you like the last movie you saw?

9.

10. What's in your lunchbox?

Students move game pieces and answer the questions or describe or identify the images. Students only move ahead if they answer the question correctly. The first person to reach "Finish," wins.

1 **Parts of a Sentence:** Circle the subject and underline the verb in each sentence.

1. She eats breakfast at 7:30 in the morning.

2. Architects design buildings.

3. She makes her bed every morning.

4. Camels live in the desert.

2 **Simple Sentences:** Which sentences have compound subjects? Which sentences have compound predicates? Check the boxes.

	compound subject	compound predicate
1. Maria and Sonia walk to school at 7:45.	☐	☐
2. Andrew rides his bike and plays soccer every day.	☐	☐
3. Don washes and dries the dishes.	☐	☐
4. My parents and I like to work in the garden.	☐	☐

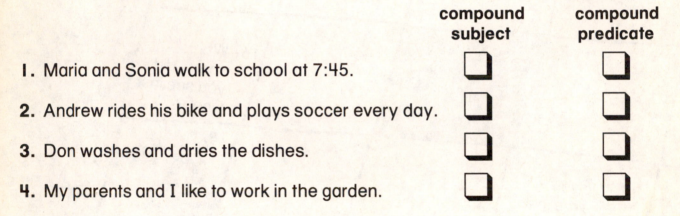

3 **Simple Sentences:** Circle the correct verb.

1. Lucy **clean** / **cleans** her room every weekend.

2. Pineapples **smell** / **smells** sweet.

3. We **is** / **are** going to the movies.

4. They **wasn't** / **weren't** in the kitchen.

4 **Kinds of Sentences:** Match. Draw a line.

1. What's the weather like today?   **a.** declarative sentence

2. Take your umbrella.   **b.** exclamatory sentence

3. I can't find my umbrella.   **c.** imperative sentence

4. Hurry! The school bus is here!   **d.** interrogative sentence

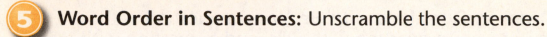
5   **Word Order in Sentences:** Unscramble the sentences.

1. cutting / is / paper / gluing / and / she

   _____

2. desk / is / the / under / cat / the

   _____

3. dining / room / a / four / table / chairs / and / are / the / in

   _____

4. help / doctors / people / well / nurses / get / and

   _____

6   **Adjectives in Sentences:** Write sentences that mean the same.

1. Monkeys' tails are long.

   _____

2. Lions have sharp teeth.

   _____

3. Hippos' mouths are very big.

   _____

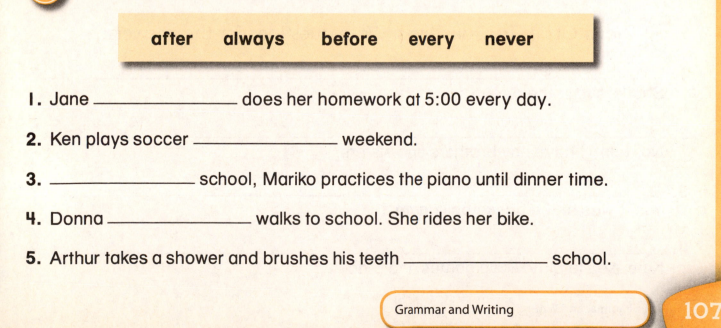

7   **Adverbs in Sentences:** Complete the sentences.

after	always	before	every	never

1. Jane _____ does her homework at 5:00 every day.

2. Ken plays soccer _____ weekend.

3. _____ school, Mariko practices the piano until dinner time.

4. Donna _____ walks to school. She rides her bike.

5. Arthur takes a shower and brushes his teeth _____ school.

8 **Word Order in Questions with *Be*:** Write a question with *is*, a question with *are*, a question with *was*, and a question with *were*. Use at least one question word.

The Verb *Be*			
question word	form of *be*	subject	rest of sentence
	Are	you	busy today?

 9 **Word Order in Questions:** Write a question with *do*, a question with *does*, and a question with *did*. Use at least one question word.

Other Verbs				
question word	auxiliary verb	subject	verb	rest of sentence
Why	did	you	miss	school yesterday?

 10 **Word Order in Questions:** Write questions for the answers.

1. _____?
Sharks live in the ocean.

2. _____?
No, I don't have any brothers and sisters.

3. _____?
Yes, I was at the basketball game.

4. _____?
Kate likes to play video games and read.